A LION WAS LEARNING TO SKI

A LION WAS LEARNING TO SKI

Ranjit Bolt

GIBSON SQUARE

This edition published for the first time by Gibson Square

UK   Tel: +44 (0)20 7096 1100
US   Tel: +1 646 216 9813

      info@gibsonsquare.com
      www.gibsonsquare.com

      ISBN 9781783340828

The moral right of Ranjit Bolt to be identified as the author of this work has been asserted in accordance with the Copyright, Designs and Patents Act 1988.

Chapter titles are typeset in font Chocolate Covered Raindrops.

Papers used by Gibson Square are natural, recyclable products made from wood grown in sustainable forests; inks used are vegetable based. Manufacturing conforms to ISO 14001, and is accredited to FSC and PEFC chain of custody schemes. Colour-printing is through a certified CarbonNeutral® company that offsets its CO2 emissions.

Printed and bound by CPI Group (UK) Ltd, Croydon, CR0 4YY

Contents

Foreword

The exact origins of the limerick are not known, but there are examples from as far back as the Middle Ages – for instance, this poem about a lion dates from the eleventh century:

> The lion is wondrous strong
> And full of the wiles of wo
> And whether he play
> Or take his prey
> He cannot do but slo. [slo = slay]

Shakespeare has limericks in some of his plays – for example, this one from Othello:

> And let me the canakin clink, clink;
> And let me the canakin clink.

A soldier's a man;
A life's but a span;
Why, then, let a soldier drink!

The name limerick of course suggests an Irish connection (Limerick being a town in Ireland) and there was certainly a group of poets in Ireland in the nineteenth century, some of them working in the town of Limerick itself, who would meet and compose limericks together, or read them to one another. Various English poets, besides Shakespeare, have experimented with the limerick. Among these are Rudyard Kipling, Alfred Lord Tennyson, and, most famously of all, the great nonsense poet, Edward Lear. Lear's limericks are rather strange, in that the final line is basically a repetition of the first. For example:

There was an Old Man with a beard,
Who said 'It is just as I feared! —
Two Owls and a Hen,
Four Larks and a Wren,
Have all built their nests in my beard!'

Some people – myself included – might consider this device to be a bit of a cheat.

I myself have been writing poetry since I was small boy. One thing I've noticed is how much people, young and old, seem to enjoy verse, especially when it makes them laugh. In fact, a rhyme can sometimes have a similar effect to a joke, particularly if the sounds are quirky, such as rhyming –onk with –lonk, or –uirk with –mirk.

My main job is a playwright, but a while ago I started writing limericks, and I decided, for fun, to make a booklet of these poems and sell them on the streets of my home town of Cambridge. The books sold like hotcakes, and people would go away reading them and chuckling to themselves. It is that little collection that forms the basis for this book.

Animals

Animals

A lion was learning to ski

In the Alps just outside Chamonix,

But he ruined his hopes

Of mastering the slopes

When he had his instructor for tea.

There was once a comedic giraffe

Whose one-liners were right off the graph,

But, though witty as heck,

It was really his neck

And its length that made everyone laugh.

An elephant trod on a flea

And the flea was as peeved as could be:

'When there's frogs and there's flies,

And there's whales your own size,

Why the heck are you picking on me?'

A cockroach was making a tour

Of a terribly poor person's floor.

The place seemed so bereft

Out of pity, it left

Its own bit of cheese by the door.

When a shark chased a diver named Rose,

She gave it a punch on the nose,

Which shoos sharks, she believed —

She was cruelly deceived,

As it robbed her of six of her toes.

There was a Scots cat called MacLeod

Who barked when he should have meowed.

This embarrassed him, yet

When a lot of cats met

At least he stood out from the crowd.

A hungry young Spanish cicada
Was poking about in his larder,
'*Ay, dios mio*!' he cried,
'I'm quite empty inside
And in all of my larder there's *nada*!'

An unmusical medic from Tring

Once was taught by a tit how to sing

And this gift he repaid

By performing first aid

On a hole that it had in its wing.

Said a man to a snake in Makamba:

'Up my wall you had better not clamber.'

Said the snake in reply

With contempt in its eye:

'I don't clamber, I glide — I'm a mamba.'

There once was an old witch of Rennes

Whose life was made miserable, when,

How she could I can't tell,

But she mis-spoke a spell

And turned herself into a hen.

Silly

A civilised felon named Franks

Had robbed branches of all the main banks.

Being a well brought up fella,

He'd send to each teller

A courteous letter of thanks.

There was once a professor named Gerda

Whose lectures were absolute murder —

Ardent lovers had tiffs,

Jolly chaps jumped off cliffs,

Just by reason of once having heard her.

There was a young lady from Derry

Who was quite inconceivably merry,

But this wasn't a freak

For she drank, every week,

Up to seventeen bottles of sherry.

A boy with a big blue balloon

Blew it up like you blow a bassoon.

And it swelled and it swelled

And he yelled and he yelled

As it carried him up to the moon.

There once was a fellow named Foley

Who ate unbelievably slowly —

It once took him a day

Just to nibble his way

Through some tacos with hot guacamole.

A costive young lady from Crewe

Had a naiad who lived in her loo

And each time she'd deposit

A voice from the closet

Cried: 'Is that the best you can do?'

A gloomy young fellow called Biff

Went and threw himself over a cliff.

'Now it's finished!' he cried

As he dropped down the side,

Then, on bouncing back up it, 'As if!'

There was a young lady from Hale

Who ate nothing but pheasant and quail

Till she woke one fine day

And remarked with dismay

That she'd sprouted a feathery tail.

A soprano who came from Penang

Would quite frequently fart when she sang.

If a match had been lit

When her top C was hit,

You'd have not heard the note for the bang.

I know of a cobbler in Crewe

Who charges a tenner a shoe.

One concession he's made is

That good-looking ladies

Can give him a cuddle in lieu.

Not so Lucky

There was a young man from Cochin

Whose toes had been made out of tin.

When he walked down the street

With no shoes on his feet

You could not hear your thoughts for

the din.

An unfortunate fellow named Futter

Had the most unbelievable stutter —

Even when in full flow

Just a Yes or a No

Took him almost a minute to utter.

A medieval lady from Leicester

In mood melancholic did fester —

She had not cracked a smile

In a heck of a while

And even her jester depressed her.

There was an Oxonian named Dodds
Whose chief pleasure was strolling round
quads.

He was strolling round Tom
When he trod on a bomb —
Well, I ask you, now what were the odds?

A miserable fellow named Durdle

Found the whole of existence a hurdle.

He would look at the day

Breaking over the bay

And his blood would immediately curdle.

There once was an old chap from Cork

Who had a peculiar walk.

He was loath to say why,

So, when asked, he'd reply

That he'd sat as a child on a fork.

An unfortunate fellow from Toft

Did a huge fart whenever he coughed.

During one bout of flu

The entire winter through

He was bodily lifted aloft.

There once was a man from Torcello

Who was such a neurotic, poor fellow,

Even stuffed to the gills

With anxiety pills

There was no one on earth so unmellow.

Fishing's pants, if I might make so bold.

I have ledgered and floated and trolled

For a week on the Cam,

Like the idiot I am,

And all that I've caught is a cold.

There once was a man from Milwaukee

Who for years was Wisconsin's top jockey,

But, with fortune and fame,

He'd no wife all the same,

For his face was all pitted and pocky.

A Buddhist from Burma opined

That suffering is all in the mind,

But he altered this view

When he sat on a screw

And it punctured his ample behind.

There was a young lady named Girder

Who committed a terrible murder.

She got clean away,

But the following day

She was shopped by a neighbour who'd

                            heard her.

A funny old fellow called Florey

Was unable to stop saying sorry

And, on being knocked down

In the centre of town,

He apologized (twice) to the lorry.

Brains

There was a man from Mull

Whose mind was slow and dull —

It was all you could do

To get twice two

Is four into his skull.

There was also a man from Staines

Who was born with the thickest of brains:

He spent five years at Eton

Was constantly beaten

And learned nothing at all for his pains.

Newton said to his helper: 'This prism'll

Never work with the weather so dismal,

And that apple that fell

Left a huge bruise as well

Christ Almighty my life is abysmal.'

In Cambridge, where yours truly dwells,

To the chiming of medieval bells,

You'll encounter a throng

Of dons ambling along

Working out how to win their Nobels.

Two bugs were discussing Man's Evil —
Whether it was acquired, or primeval —
'I've no views on that head',
The wiser one said,
'I'm just thankful I'm only a weevil.'

Abroad

There was an old man from Rabat

Who purchased a pink rubber mat,

But, possessing no floor,

He would fold it in four

And employ it instead as a hat.

One fine morning, the folk of Tralee

Were convinced that they'd heard a banshee,

But it wasn't a fay

It was Paddy O'Shea

Who'd been stung on the bum by a bee.

A guy from LA called Jim Fox

Weighed two seventy pounds in his socks.

As he headed their way

You would hear people say:

'Is that Jim, or some fresh seismic shocks?'

There was a young man from Berlin

Who believed that to breathe was a sin

And, by hook or by brook,

For each breath that he took

He would hold the next seventy in.

When the Empire was still fairly young

In the spirit from whence it had sprung,

The intrepid explorers

Ate mouldy pakoras

Off plates made of elephant dung.

There was a young man from Dunkirk

Who was simply an out and out berk —

I would try to evoke

All the faults of this bloke

But no words that I know of would work.

There was also a man from Bombay

Whose appallingness blew one away —

If I sought to appraise

All his terrible traits

It would take me a year and a day.

An Italian lady named Lisa

Was a truly exceptional sneezer.

One particular sneeze

Was as loud as you please

And propelled her from Florence to Pisa.

Long ago in Provence an old man

Owned an 'Apples and Pears' by Cézanne,

And how peeved are his heirs

That those apples and pears

Were employed to repair a divan.

?

A Paddy whose county was Cork
Was incredibly partial to pork.
If you went to Fermoy
You might well see this boy
With a chop on the end of his fork.

There was once a Bengali mahout

Whose elephant gave him the boot.

And I don't mean the sack,

But a kick in the back

That propelled him as far as Beirut.

A young Carolinian named Trigger

For a very short while was a digger.

He'd have wrought transformation

Throughout the whole nation

If only his spade had been bigger.

A young single woman from Beaune

Got fed up of being on her own —

It was doing her head

So she went and got wed.

Now she'd kill for one minute alone.

It is not common knowledge,

                                   but Spooner,

When he dined at a restaurant in Poona,

Ordered one khev samani,

A bamb liryani,

Dana chal and a hot bicken chuna.

An old sadhu who lived in the Ghats

Had twelve monkeys and seventeen cats

He'd've given an arm

To make them keep calm

But they jabbered and screeched

and had spats

Acknowledgements

I would like to express my gratitude to my friend James Essinger, of Canterbury Literary Agency, for taking on this collection, and to my editor, Martin Rynja, for his commitment and enthusiasm, not say patience!